Pocket Guide

About this Pocket Guide

SQL Server 2012 contains a plethora of new features and functionality centered around three pillars: Mission Critical Confidence, Breakthrough Insight, and Cloud on Your Terms. This pocket guide is designed to give a quick review of most of the key features within these three pillars as well as provide useful reference information on licensing.

If you have any comments or suggestions please feel free to contact the author at Robert.Walters@Microsoft.com.

About the Author

Robert Walters is a Data Platform Technology Specialist for Microsoft in the Northeast district. His extensive experience with Microsoft SQL Server began over 12 years ago when he worked as a consultant for Microsoft Consulting Services in Denver, Colorado. Shortly after the dot-com bubble burst, Mr. Walters returned to Microsoft's headquarters and worked as a program manager in the SQL Server product unit. There, he owned various features within SQL Server including SQL Server Agent, various management features, and the security for the database engine. Walters has co-authored three patents for technologies used within SQL Server.

Mr. Walters has also co-authored Programming Microsoft SQL Server 2005 by Microsoft Press, and Pro SQL Server 2005 by Apress Publishing. He was the lead author of Accelerated SQL Server 2008, Beginning SQL Server 2008 Administration and Beginning SQL Server 2012 Administration by Apress. He holds a bachelor's of science degree in Electrical Engineering from Michigan State University and a master's degree in business administration from Seattle University.

SQL Server 2012 Pocket Guide   Revision 1.2 - 3/8/12

TABLE OF CONTENTS

SQL Server 2012 Pocket Guide   **3**

APPENDIX B: LICENSING DATASHEET 81

Introducing SQL Server 2012

Over the years, Microsoft has evolved the SQL Server product from a relational database engine to a complete data management platform. Today SQL Server customers are managing petabytes of data and witnessing 100,000+ transactions per second throughput all at an affordable total cost of ownership. SQL Server 2012 is the latest and most significant release of Microsoft's database platform. In this pocket guide we will discuss the mission critical enhancements to SQL Server including how to achieve your 9's with AlwaysOn High Availability.

Native business intelligence capabilities have existed in SQL Server since the days of SQL Server 7.0. With each new edition came leap frog advancements in analytical processing and data mining. The result of all this investment comes with Microsoft now being defined as a leader in the Gartner magic quadrant for Business Intelligence platforms. SQL Server 2012 builds upon this success and allows users to discover new insights into data through rapid data exploration and visualization. Server 2012 works with data from all sources including unstructured, structured, and cloud. In this latest version of SQL Server, Microsoft has continued the theme of self-service Business Intelligence.

Edition Changes

SQL Server 2012 comes in three main editions: Enterprise, Business Intelligence and Standard. Each edition is built from the same solid code base with differences in editions coming from the feature set exposed and intentional technical limitations set within each specific edition.

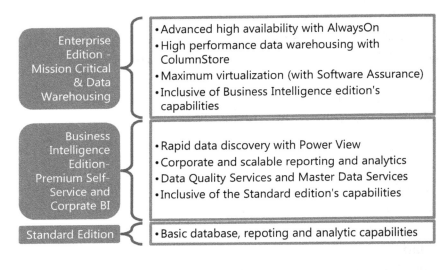

Enterprise Edition - Mission Critical & Data Warehousing
- Advanced high availability with AlwaysOn
- High performance data warehousing with ColumnStore
- Maximum virtualization (with Software Assurance)
- Inclusive of Business Intelligence edition's capabilities

Business Intelligence Edition- Premium Self-Service and Corprate BI
- Rapid data discovery with Power View
- Corporate and scalable reporting and analytics
- Data Quality Services and Master Data Services
- Inclusive of the Standard edition's capabilities

Standard Edition
- Basic database, repoting and analytic capabilities

Enterprise Edition is designed for Mission Critical and Data Warehousing applications. This edition contains all the features and functionality available with SQL Server with no imposed technical limitations. The Business Intelligence edition is a subset of Enterprise edition and is designed to provide a premium self-service business intelligence solution for your organization. Key enhancements like Power View which allows for rapid data discovery are included in this edition. Standard edition is a subset of Business Intelligence edition and provides basic database, reporting and analytic capabilities. The table below shows a feature comparison among the three main editions:

Capabilities	Enterprise	Business Intelligence	Standard
Maximum Number of Cores	OS Max*	16 Cores-DB OS Max-BI	16 Cores
Basic OLTP	✓	✓	✓
Programmability (T-SQL, Spatial Support, FileTable)	✓	✓	✓
Manageability (SQL Server Management Studio, Policy-based Management)	✓	✓	✓
Corporate Business Intelligence (Reporting, Analytics, Multidimensional BI Semantic Model)	✓	✓	✓
Self-Service Business Intelligence (Alerting, Power View, PowerPivot for SharePoint Server)	✓	✓	

Enterprise data management *(Data Quality Services, Master Data Services)*	✓	✓	
In-Memory Tabular BI Semantic Model	✓	✓	
Advanced Security *(Advanced auditing, transparent data encryption)*	✓		
Data Warehousing *(ColumnStore, compression, partitioning)*	✓		
High availability *(AlwaysOn)*	Advanced	Basic**	Basic**

*SQL Server 2012 Enterprise Edition server licenses - whether newly purchased or upgraded with Software Assurance - will be subject to a 20 core per server license maximum. See the Licensing section of this pocket guide for more information on licensing changes.

**Basic includes 2 node Failover Clustering.

In case you are wondering where Web, Developer and Express editions are you can be rest assured that these specialized editions will still exist in SQL Server 2012.

There is another version of SQL Server that is new to SQL Server 2012. This version called SQL Server 2012 Express LocalDB (LocalDB) is targeted at the developer and is a lightweight version of SQL Server Express edition. Some may think SQL Server Express is already light weight but it still runs as a service and requires network configuration to make work. LocalDB has all the programmability of SQL Server Express with zero configuration as it runs in user mode not as a Windows service. For more information on LocalDB check out the following URL: http://go.microsoft.com/fwlink/?LinkId=221201.

This remainder of this pocket guide will cover these capabilities and more. Remember with SQL Server there are no costly add-ons to purchase. Features and functionality are only bound to the edition that you utilize. If you are interested in a more detailed list of features within each edition see the "Features Supported by the Editions" in Appendix A.

Mission-Critical Confidence

A Mission Critical environment is one where your business will typically suffer financial loss if services are not available. Microsoft's value of SQL Server is mission critical performance at a low total cost of ownership. A case study by Alinean entitled, "Microsoft SQL Server and Oracle Database: A comparative study on Total Cost of Administration" found that the annual cost for administering a database on the Microsoft platform was $1,605 versus $7,385 of an Oracle database. This is a 460% difference. Combine this low TCO and the fact that Microsoft has proven itself repeatedly in delivering the required 9's and performance its customers demand and you'll see why Microsoft DBAs run more mission critical databases, when compared to Oracle DBAs. For more

information on the Alinean case study check out the following URL:
http://www.alinean.com/PDFs/Microsoft_SQL_Server_and_O racle-Alinean_TCA_Study_2010.pdf.

Availability and data protection with AlwaysOn

SQL Server 2012 builds upon the successful planned and unplanned downtime features found in earlier versions and introduces a new enterprise-level highly available and disaster recovery solution called AlwaysOn Availability Groups. To fully understand Availability Groups, let's first review a feature called Database Mirroring.

Database Mirroring was first introduced in SQL Server 2005 as a way to automatically ship transactions from a primary to a secondary server. DBAs could use Database Mirroring as a way to failover a particular database instead of the entire server instance as is the case with Failover Clustering. Database Mirroring supported automatic client failover with some minor changes to client application code. One of the limitations with Database Mirroring is that you could only have one secondary server so effectively only one failover location per database. If your application used more than one database managing the failover was a bit more difficult since each database mirror was independent of any other on the server instance. One of the most common feature requests for Database Mirroring is the ability to use the secondary server's copy of the database for something useful. When Database Mirroring is running you have a duplicate copy available on a running on the secondary SQL Server instance. However, you cannot make a connection to this secondary database because the database is in restore only mode so that it can load the transactions as they are sent from the primary server. Given these issues with Database Mirroring, Microsoft invested heavily in this feature and developed a new feature called AlwaysOn Availability Groups that is similar to Database Mirroring but addresses a lot of these shortcomings.

Offload work to secondary servers

An AlwaysOn Availability Group is a collection of one or more databases that can failover together. This group of databases is known as an availability group. An availability group can have up to four secondary replicas or possible failover targets.

The secondary replicas can be asynchronous or synchronously written to. You can mix and match these but you can only synchronously write to three replicas.

By default the secondary replica databases are in restore-only mode but you can change this and allow active read-only connections. This allows you to off-load workloads like database backup and reporting to these secondary servers. Query performance on the secondary is tuned since SQL Server automatically creates and updates statistics on the readable secondary. These temporary statistics are stored in the TempDB on the secondary server and require no physical changes in user database. In the end, the query can generate optimal query plans on the readable secondary replicas.

Automatic redirection of client connections occurs by leveraging an availability group listener. The availability group listener is associated with a unique DNS name that serves as a virtual network name and one or more virtual IP addresses. Thus, there is no need for the developer or administrator to tell each client connection the primary and secondary server names. Upon a failover, the client who is connected to the virtual IP of the availability group listener will simply be redirected to the secondary replica.

Unlike Database Mirroring, there is no need for a witness server. The inter-node health detection and automatic failover capability exist because SQL Server uses these capabilities within Windows Server Failover Clustering. When you set up an Availability Group each SQL Server instance that is part of the group will be a part of the same Windows Server cluster. If you are concerned about configuring shared disks and all the hassle that comes with that don't be as Availability Groups do not need shared disks. Setup from a Windows Server Failover Clustering perspective is very straightforward.

AlwaysOn Availability Groups eliminate idle hardware and improve IT cost efficiency and performance.

Adding value to your clustered environment

Geo-clustering or multi-subnet clustering is the concept where we have our active and passive nodes on a different subnet that is most likely geographically separated. While setting up this type of clustering was possible in Windows Server 2003, Windows Server 2008 R2 natively supports

such a scenario. However, up until SQL Server 2012, SQL Server didn't leverage the new multi-site clustering capabilities.

SQL Server 2012 introduces an improved failure detection and failure condition level property that allows you to define a more flexible policy. Technically, a server restart or failover should be triggered if any of these conditions are raised:

• SQL Server service is down

• SQL Server is not responsive (Resource DLL cannot receive data from sp_server_diagnostics)

• System stored procedure sp_server_diagnostics returns 'system error'

• System stored procedure sp_server_diagnostics returns 'resource error'

• System stored procedure sp_server_diagnostics returns 'query_processing error'

By setting the server configuration property **FailureConditionLevel** you can define when a failover should occur. The T-SQL syntax to change this property is as follows:

ALTER SERVER CONFIGURATION SET FAILOVER CLUSTER PROPERTY FailureConditionLevel = <failover level>;

For example, setting the property to "0" indicates that no failover or restart will be triggered automatically on any failure conditions. This level is best used for system maintenance purposes only. Setting the property to "3" indicates that a server restart or failover will be triggered if the SQL Server service is down, SQL Server is not responsive (Resource DLL cannot receive data from sp_server_diagnostics) and the system stored procedure sp_server_diagnostics returns 'system error'. For a complete list of the five settings see the SQL Server Books Online article, "Failover Policy for Failover Cluster Instances" located at the following URL: http://msdn.microsoft.com/en-us/library/ff878664(v=sql.110).aspx#determine.

Another exciting improvement to SQL Server 2012 is **tempdb** can now be written to a local disk when SQL Server is part of a cluster. This may yield much better performance for **tempdb** heavy workloads in a cluster especially when you use solid state drives.

Maintain uptime with Windows Server Core

SQL Server 2012 can be installed on Windows Server Core. This edition of Windows Server is slimmer with most of its weight reducing having to do with its lacks of a graphical user interface or tools. By not having a lot of the GUI based tools and functions mean you will see about a 50-60% reduction in the number of operating system patches to your SQL Server environments. Running on Windows Server Core also means that you may need less memory per guest when running inside a hypervisor. This allows you to run more SQL Server virtual machines per host.

High Availability for StreamInsight

StreamInsight provides complex event processing capabilities to SQL Server. CEP is used when you need to quickly look for certain patterns in data and the process of saving the data to a database is too slow. Think about the stock market and analyzing the change of the price of stocks. Monitoring Key Performance Indicators based on all these data is something prime for a CEP solution. In SQL Server 2012, new checkpoint capabilities were added which adds resilience against planned and unplanned downtimes. In addition user-defined streams were introduced which provide predictive modeling and pattern matching. Performance monitor counters were also added to improve the monitoring and administration of the CEP solution.

SQL Server Management pack

SQL Server 2012 will have a management pack for System Center Operations Manager (SCOM). This management pack will contain information relating to Availability Groups and AlwaysOn tasks. It will have native Policy-based management integration allowing you to pull you policies right into System Center Operations Manager and be alerted on failures. The management pack also has additional rules for replication and enhanced database mirroring support.

Increase performance with columnstore index

A columnstore index is a new type of index that improves data warehouse queries by hundreds to thousands of times. This new index is created and managed through familiar T-SQL syntax and is fully compatible with all reporting solutions like SQL Server Reporting Services. A columnstore index reaps this great performance because it stores each column in a separate set of disk pages as opposed to storing multiple rows per page which is the traditional way to store data within a database file.

By having data stored in the columns this yields the following benefits:

- Only the columns needed to solve the query are fetched from the disk
- Data compression is easier due to the redundancy of data within the column
- Buffer hit rates are improved since data is highly compressed and frequently accessed parts of common used columns remain in memory while infrequently parts are paged out

Members of the SQL Server product team produced a whitepaper called, "Column Store Indexes for Fast Data Warehouse Query Processing in SQL Server 11.0" published November 2010. This whitepaper is located at the following URL:
http://download.microsoft.com/download/8/C/1/8C1CE06B
-DE2F-40D1-9C5C-
3EE521C25CE9/Columnstore%20Indexes%20for%20Fast%2

[0DW%20QP%20SQL%20Server%2011.pdf](#). In this paper they describe a test scenario of a 1TB test data warehouse with a fact table containing 1.44 billion rows. On a 32-logical processor server with 256GB of RAM they achieved these performance metrics:

	Total CPU time (seconds)	Elapsed time (seconds)
Columnstore	31.0	1.10
No columnstore	502	501
Speed increase	16X	455X

Although you can create a columnstore index on any table the sweet spot is data that is a fact table or a read-only table. From the performance results above you can see the huge performance gains made from simply defining an index on the columns. For more information check out the whitepaper listed above.

Enhancing your secure SQL Server environment

SQL Server is the most secure database platform of the major database vendors today. This achievement came as a result of a major shift in internal software engineering processes back in the early 2000's. Currently the process for a particular new feature within the product consists of threat models, data flow diagrams, and developer code reviews to name a few. For more information on how SQL Server security relates to the rest of the industry check out this whitepaper entitled, "SQL Server is the industry leading database" located that this URL: http://download.microsoft.com/download/9/8/5/98591434 -2E0B-472F-8084- 4C73661ABA4E/ITIC%20Microsoft%20SQL%20Server%20Se curity%20Final%209%208%2010.pdf

Achieving separation of duties with user-defined server roles

Historically if you wanted to grant a database login permissions at a server level you could either add that login to one of a few fixed server roles like **backupadmin** or **sysadmin** role. Starting with SQL Server 2005 you could explicitly grant a server level permission like CONTROL SERVER to a particular login. This enables some scenarios but most organizations do not manage every login and database user individually, rather, they tend to use roles. In SQL Server 2012 database administrators can create roles that are scoped at the server instance level. These user-defined server roles allow you to create a role, add logins and grant instance level permissions. One of the biggest benefits is that we can create a sysadmin like role without having to grant sysadmin privileges. For example, let's create a server level role called, DBA Role as follows:

CREATE SERVER ROLE [DBA Role]

Next we define what permissions this new role is assigned and add the necessary DENY permissions to restrict the user from changing audits or impersonating the auditor.

Note that even though we granted CONTROL SERVER which is almost sysadmin, SQL Server will obey a DENY even when the user has been granted CONTROL SERVER permission.

GRANT CONTROL SERVER TO [DBA Role]

GO

DENY ALTER ANY SERVER AUDIT TO [DBA Role]

GO

DENY ALTER ANY LOGIN TO [DBA Role]

GO

DENY IMPERSONATE ON LOGIN::CorporateAuditor TO [DBA Role]

GO

To add a login to a user-defined server role we issue the ALTER SERVER ROLE statement as follows:

ALTER SERVER ROLE [DBA Role] ADD MEMBER [Julie]

In this example, Julie is a member of the DBA Role, she can do anything that CONTROL SERVER can do except impersonate the CorporateAuditor login, alter any login on the server and alter any server audit.

Auditing support on all editions of SQL Server

All editions of SQL Server 2012 allow you to create a server level specification audit. This allows you to leverage the native auditing capabilities for all SQL Server servers in your enterprise and audit events like failed logins. The Enterprise edition will contain more fine grained auditing including the ability to audit SELECT, INSERT, UPDATE, DELETE and EXECUTE statements against specific objects within the database.

Create application specific events with user-defined audits

Sometimes your database application uses a single connection to the database server. In this architecture it is not easy to audit a user because there is just one user always connecting to the database. To mitigate this scenario, you can now raise your own user-defined audit event from within your database application. To create a user-defined event simply use the **sp_audit_write** stored procedure as follows:

EXEC sp_audit_write

@user_defined_event_id = 27,

@succeeded = 1,

@user_defined_information = N'Web user: John Doe successfully logged in.' ;

GO

Increased audit resilience

SQL Server 2012 introduced the "continue" option when handing an audit write failure. This option allows the operation that caused the audit event to continue. Additional code robustness was added to mitigate temporary network outages and disk issues.

Default Schema for Windows Groups

Schemas within SQL Server allow you to group objects together. There is an owner for a schema and it's easy to change ownership. There is also a default schema that is used for each database user when the user does not select a schema for a requested object. When the user was authenticated to SQL Server via a Windows Group and not a specific login it was not possible to provide a default schema. SQL Server 2012 provides the ability to define a default schema for windows groups connecting to SQL Server.

Contained Database authentication

In SQL Server 2012 a partially contained database is one that contains the authentication information for the database users. It is considered partial because there is still some information stored in other databases like master and msdb that is used by the database. With a contained database users only exist in the context of the database itself. When connected they can't see master, msdb or change to any other database context because their account doesn't exist in these databases.

To create a contained database you must first enable the "contained database authentication" system option as follows:

SP_CONFIGURE 'show advanced options', 1

RECONFIGURE

GO

SP_CONFIGURE 'contained database authentication', 1

RECONFIGURE WITH OVERRIDE

GO

Next, we set the containment of this database to partial.

CREATE DATABASE Sales

GO

ALTER DATABASE Sales SET CONTAINMENT=PARTIAL;

Now that our database is set to partially contained we can create database users directly without any associated SQL logins. These users can be created with a password or they can be Windows principals. If you use a Windows principal they do not need any existing access to SQL Server. For this example, assume we have created a local Windows User named, "John" on the server, "SQLPROD1". To create both a user with a password and a user from a Windows principal we issue the following commands:

USE Sales

GO

CREATE USER [Rob] WITH PASSWORD='pass@word1';

GO

CREATE USER [SQLPROD1\John];

GO

Cryptographic enhancements

AES256 is now used to secure the database master key, symmetric keys and other objects within SQL Server. There is no more use of Triple DES for these purposes. Also, password hashes now use SHA512.

Simulate Production workloads

Distributed Replay provides the ability to simulate production workloads. The ability to simulate workloads is key in application upgrade testing and configuration change testing scenarios. SQL Server 2012 Distributed Replay is a multi-client scalability feature that enables multiple low cost clients (workstations) to handle large workload traces within reasonable time. The typical physical Distributed Replay environment consists of the following:

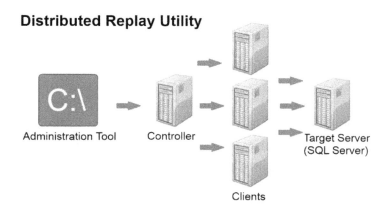

The Distributed Replay administration tool is a console application, DReplay.exe. It is used to communicate with the distributed replay controller. The Distributed Replay controller orchestrates the actions of the distributed replay clients. There can only be one controller instance in each

Distributed Replay environment. Each Distributed Replay client can be either a physical or virtual machine. Together these clients work together to simulate workloads against the Target Server.

Resource Governor enhancements

SQL Server 2012 support larger scale multi-tenancy environment by increasing maximum number of resource pools to 64. A Database Administrators can also enable a cap on CPU usage. This feature enables a predicable chargeback and user isolation scenario.

There is a new DMV, **sys.dm_resource_govenor_resource_pool_affinity**, which tracks resource pool affinity. A Resource pool can be affinitized to individual or groups of schedulers.

Database Recovery made simple

The database recovery advisor within the SQL Server Management Studio Restore Database dialog can help you when restoring a database to a point in time. The advisor provides a visual timeline for you to select down to the second when you want to restore the data. The advisor then generates the necessary commands and tasks to get the database back to the specific time. If this has to include an additional backup of the tail of the log or setting the database to single user mode it does this as well.

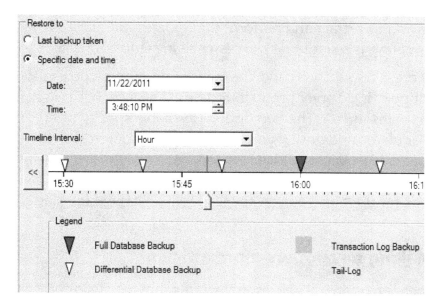

Also, if you have a corrupt database page you can now restore that particular page from a backup.

Replace legacy SQL Trace with Extended Events

For its time SQL Trace was a great tool used capture activity against a SQL Server instance. SQL Server 2008 introduced Extended Events as a complement to SQL Server Trace. Microsoft has formally deprecated SQL Trace in SQL Server 2012 and has added management tools support for Extended Events in SQL Server management studio.

Install latest updates directly from setup

Setup can now check for any product updates. This allows setup or the entire product to be updated without you having to extract and perform the updates manually. Updating is a single click experience in setup UI.

There is also a command line switch added to setup.exe to support SQL Server product updates. The switch is called "updatesource". The two options available specify where to look for updates. If you select, "Updatesource:MU" this checks with Microsoft Update service. You can also specify a UNC or folder path directly. If you do not want setup to look for updates you can specify the UpdateEnabled=false parameter.

Making developers more efficient

There are many T-SQL improvements that will delight DBAs and developers.

Paging support

Imagine if you have a recordset that contains a few thousand results and the front end of this is a web page application. The web user wants to page through the results 100 items at a time. Without native paging support you would either have to return the entire result set and handle the paging at the presentation layer or write a complex queries to obtain the specific rows for that requested range. In SQL Server 2012 you can write a query that returns just the block of rows you are seeking. For example, this query will return rows 51-61 within the result set:

SELECT product_name. product_price FROM ProductInventory

  ORDER BY product_name ASC

    OFFSET (50) ROWS   FETCH NEXT 10 ROWS ONLY

Sequences

When you create a table with a primary key you want to have a unique number or identity for each row. Traditionally SQL Server users leveraged the IDENTITY property which is used to create an identity column. The problem with using the identity column is that it is only bound to that particular table in that particular database. If you are sharing this identity across multiple sites or applications the values may conflict. For this and other reasons, there is now in SQL Server 2012 a sequence object. To create a SEQUENCE object you can issue the following T-SQL statement:

CREATE SEQUENCE PetFoodIDSequence

  AS INT

  START WITH 10

  INCREMENT BY 1

To leverage the SEQUENCE, use the following:

CREATE TABLE PetFood

(pet_food INT DEFAULT (NEXT VALUE FOR PetFoodIDSequence),

 food_brand VARCHAR (20));

GO

If you want to take a look at the current value you can query the sys.sequences catalog view as follows:

SELECT current_value FROM sys.sequences WHERE name='PetFoodIDSequence'

A better way to THROW errors

SQL Server 2005 introduced a TRY/CATCH block which was loosely related to the .NET implementation. This allows T-SQL developers to group code within a TRY block and if an error occurs, the CATCH block of code would be executed. The THROW statement is introduced in SQL Server 2012 as an alternative to the RAISERROR statement. While each has their pros and cons, THROW should be considered as the primary way to raise user-defined exceptions in your T-SQL code.

THROW allows ad-hoc error text. It does not require you to have user messages pre-defined in sys.messages.

THROW can also be used within a CATCH block to re-throw the same error. This allows the calling application to also process same error. Consider the following code:

```
CREATE TABLE MyErrorLog(ErrorTimeStamp DATETIME2,
ErrorSeverity INT, ErrorMessage VARCHAR(MAX))
GO
BEGIN TRY
  DECLARE @num INT = 1 / 0;
END TRY
BEGIN CATCH
```

INSERT INTO MyErrorLog VALUES(SYSDATETIME(), ERROR_SEVERITY(), ERROR_MESSAGE());

THROW;

END CATCH

Upon execution SQL Server will return the following:

```
Msg 8134, Level 16, State 1, Line 2
Divide by zero error encountered.
```

If we look into our MyErrorLog table we would see our inserted data:

ErrorTimeStamp	ErrorSeverity	ErrorMessage
2011-11-23 06:.. encountered.	16	Divide by zero error

Metadata discovery

In SQL Server 2012 if you want to review metadata of a one of more T-SQL statements you can use the new sp_describe_first_result_set statement. This statement returns metadata for the first possible result set of the T-SQL that you provide. Given our previous example with the MyErrorLog table, if we issue the following statement:

Sp_describe_first_result_set N'SELECT * FROM MyErrorLog'

This would return a result set that includes a large number of informative columns. Information such as the column name, ordinal location, if it's nullable, the data type, maximum length, precision, scale, collation, and many others. For a complete list check out the SQL Server Books Online topic, "sp_decribe_first_result_set (Transact-SQL)"

located at the following URL:
http://msdn.microsoft.com/en-
us/library/ff878602(v=SQL.110).aspx.

PARSE

PARSE returns the result of an expression translated into
the requested data type. This is useful when converting
from string to date/time and number types. You should
continue to use CAST or COVERT for general type
conversions.

SELECT PARSE('€345,98' AS money USING 'de-DE') AS Result

The result would be as follows:

Result
345.98

TRY_PARSE

TRY_PARSE is similar to PARSE except that it will return a
NULL if the cast fails.

SELECT TRY_PARSE('BlahBlahBlah' AS DATETIME2 USING 'en-US') AS Result

The result would be as follows:

Result
NULL

TRY_CONVERT

TRY_CONVERT is similar to CONVERT except that it will
return NULL if the conversion fails.

```
SELECT
    CASE WHEN TRY_CONVERT(float,'test') IS NULL
    THEN 'Cast failed'
    ELSE 'Cast succeeded'
END AS Result;
GO
```

The result would be as follows:

Result
Case failed

Seven new Date and Time functions

SQL Server 2012 adds seven new functions to support date and time. Their use and results are self-explanatory. The following is a demo script with the results shown in the comment field after the statement :

```
SELECT DATEFROMPARTS(2010, 12, 31)
--2010-12-31
SELECT DATETIME2FROMPARTS ( 2010, 12, 31, 23, 59, 59, 0, 0 )
AS Result;
--2010-12-31 23:59:59
SELECT DATETIMEFROMPARTS (2010, 12, 31, 23, 59, 59, 0)
--2010-12-31 23:59:59.000
SELECT DATETIMEOFFSETFROMPARTS (2010, 12, 31, 14, 23, 36, 0, 12, 0, 7)
--2010-12-31 14:23:36.0000000 +12:00
```

SELECT SMALLDATETIMEFROMPARTS (2010, 12, 31, 23, 59)

--2010-12-31 23:59:00

SELECT TIMEFROMPARTS (23, 59, 59, 1234567, 7)

--23:59:59.1234567

The EOMONTH function returns the last day of the month that contains the specified date, with an optional offset.

DECLARE @date DATETIME;

SET @date = '12/1/2010';

SELECT EOMONTH (@date) AS Result;

The result would be as follows:

2010-12-31

Leap year is also supported, SELECT EOMONTH('2/1/2012') would yield the answer 2012-02-29.

CHOOSE

CHOOSE returns the item at the specified index from the list of values.

For example, consider the following script:

SELECT CHOOSE (3, 'Manager', 'Director', 'Developer', 'Tester') AS Result;

The result set would be as follows:

Result
Developer

IIF

IIF returns one of two values depending on whether the Boolean expression evaluates to true or false.

DECLARE @a int = 45;

DECLARE @b int = 40;

SELECT IIF (@a > @b, 'TRUE', 'FALSE') AS Result;

The result set would be as follows:

Result
TRUE

CONCAT

CONCAT will return a string that is the concatenation of two or more string values.

SELECT CONCAT ('Happy ', 'Birthday ', 12, '/', NULL,'25') AS Result;

The result set would be as follows:

Result
Happy Birthday 12/25

Note that null values are ignored.

Eight new built-in analytic functions

Analytic functions are used to compute moving averages, running totals, percentages or top-N results within a group. SQL Server 2012 introduces the following analytic functions:

Function	Description
CUME_DIST	Computes the relative position of a specified value in a group of values.
FIRST_VALUE	Returns the first value in an ordered set of values.
LAG	Provides access to previous rows in the result set without the need to use self-join.
LAST_VALUE	Returns the last value in an ordered set of values
LEAD	Provides access to rows that follow the current row in the result set without the need to use self-join.

PERCENTILE_CONT	Calculates a percentile based on a continuous distribution of the column value.
PERCENTILE_DISC	Computes a specific percentile for sorted values in an entire rowset or within distinct partitions of a rowset.
PERCENT_RANK	Calculates the relative rank of a row within a group of rows. Use to evaluate the relative standing of a value within a query result set or partition.

For a complete description of these functions including examples of their use see the SQL Server Books Online Topic, "Analytic Functions (Transact-SQL)" located at the following URL: http://msdn.microsoft.com/en-us/library/hh213234(v=SQL.110).aspx.

SET LANGUAGE

SET LANGUAGE specifies the language environment for the current session. By changing this you affect datetime formats and system messages. For example, consider the following script:

```
DECLARE @old_lang VARCHAR(32) = @@LANGUAGE
```

```
DECLARE @new_lang VARCHAR(32) = 'German'
```

```
SET LANGUAGE @new_lang
```

```
SELECT DATENAME(WEEKDAY, SYSDATETIME())
```

```
SET LANGUAGE @old_lang
```

The result set would be as follows:

```
Die Spracheneinstellung wurde auf Deutsch geändert.
-----------------------------
Mittwoch
(1 row(s) affected)
Changed language setting to us_english.
```

Improved Dynamic SQL

Dynamic SQL is not all bad. For security reasons you need to make sure you practice good coding skills and use parameters where appropriate. SQL Server 2012 adds support for defining a contract for returned result sets. When used with dynamic SQL this adds another layer of protection from rogue SQL statements. To help illustrate this consider the following script:

```
CREATE TABLE #Customers (CustomerID INT, Name
VARCHAR(50), IsActiveCustomer BIT)
```

```
GO
```

```
INSERT INTO #Customers VALUES(1,'Rob',1), (2,'Julie',1)
```

```
GO
```

In this example our SELECT statement returns two columns but our contract only requests one.

DECLARE @SQL VARCHAR(50)='SELECT Name,IsActiveCustomer FROM #Customers'

EXEC(@SQL)

WITH RESULT SETS

((Name VARCHAR(50))   );

The following error will result from the above statement:

> *Msg 11537, Level 16, State 1, Line 1*
> *EXECUTE statement failed because its WITH RESULT SETS clause specified 1 column(s) for result set number 1, but the statement sent 2 column(s) at run time.*

In this example our contract calls for a column of type BIT to be returned.

DECLARE @SQL VARCHAR(50)='SELECT Name FROM #Customers'

EXEC(@SQL)

WITH RESULT SETS

((IsActive BIT)   );

The following error will result from the above statement:

> *Msg 8114, Level 16, State 2, Line 1*
> *Error converting data type varchar(50) to bit.*

In this example, the statement and the contract both expect the same column number and data type.

DECLARE @SQL VARCHAR(50)='SELECT Name FROM #Customers'

```
EXEC(@SQL)
WITH RESULT SETS
(        (Name VARCHAR(50))        );
```

The following results are found from the above statement:

```
Name
-------------------
Rob
Julie
```

Creating a database file system with FileTable

Traditionally the maximum amount of data you could store
in a single column of a row is 2GB. Given this constraint
what if you didn't know the maximum size of the object
you wanted to store or you knew it was more than 2GB.
Most developers would simply store a file pointer to the
object which would be stored somewhere on a file system.
There were a few challenges with this approach. The
developer needed to make sure the application could get
access to the file since it was stored outside of SQL Server.
Also, there is no referential integrity between the database
and the file system. Someone could modify or delete the
file and the pointer would still exist in the database.
Likewise, the pointer in the database could be updated or
deleted.   These problems were mostly solved with the
FILESTREAM feature in SQL Server 2008. In FILESTREAM
you create a file group and store your objects directly in
the table as you normally would with other data.
FILESTREAM data can be accessed directly from Windows
API or from T-SQL. The data you store can be as big as the

volume you defined the file group on potentially far exceeded the old 2GB limit. One added benefit now is that when you backup the database, the data that is stored in the FILESTREAM file group is also backed up. Upon failover this data exists on the secondary site as well.

FileTable is the next iteration of the FILESTREAM feature. FileTable lets an application integrate its storage and relational data components and builds on top of the FILESTREAM technology. With FILESTREAM, to use the Windows API to fetch the data you had to obtain a transaction context ID. With FileTable its seamless you do not have to do special coding to obtain the data using the Windows API. FileTables are exposed as network shares. Users who have explicit access to this share can seamlessly copy/paste/update without having to connect to SQL Server and use T-SQL. FileTable exposes all the properties found in NTFS.

To illustrate FileTable, let's create a FileTable to store photos. Note in order to define a filestream filegroup you will need to enable the filesteam feature in SQL Server. If you did not do this upon installing of the SQL Server instance you can enable it through the Properties of the SQL Server instance in the SQL Server Computer Manager. Also, we need to make sure the destination folder, C:\Demo\FileTable is already created for this particular demo script to work.

```
CREATE DATABASE ContosoDigital

ON PRIMARY

(name=ContosoDigital_File,

FILENAME=N'C:\Demo\FileTable\ContosoDigital.mdf'),

FILEGROUP SQLStorage CONTAINS FILESTREAM

(name=ContosoDigital_Filestream_File,

FILENAME=N'C:\Demo\FileTable\ContosoDigital_FileSteram')

WITH FILESTREAM (non_transacted_access=full,
directory_name=N'PhotoContent')

--With the database created we can now create the Photos
table, notice the special

--syntax of "AS FILETABLE" this causes a table created with a
fixed schema.

USE ContosoDigital

GO

CREATE TABLE Photos AS FILETABLE WITH
(filetable_directory=N'PhotoLibrary')

GO
```

If you look at Object Explorer and navigate down to the ContosoDigital Databases container node you will see two nodes for Tables: System Tables and FileTables.

Also note that when the Photos table was created, SQL Server included a bunch of columns for us. Some of these columns are the same as the attributes for an NTFS file and folder.

Now let's create a folder called, "Birthday Photos" using the following code:

INSERT INTO Photos (name,is_directory) VALUES ('Birthday Photos',1)

We create this using T-SQL but we can also navigate to the file share created by right clicking the Photos table and selecting, "Explore FileTable Directory".

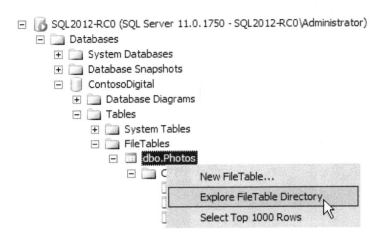

This will launch Windows Explorer shown in the following screen capture:

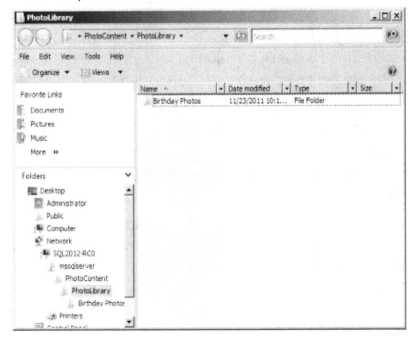

Notice that we can add files and folders from within Windows Explorer. Assume that we added a birthday photo to the "Birthday Photos" directory. We can now launch the picture right from the folder using Windows Explorer or access it via T-SQL by simply SELECTing the Photos table.

Semantic Search

By extracting and indexing statistically relevant key phrases, SQL Server's Semantic Search feature provides deep insight into unstructured documents stored in SQL Server databases. SQL Server uses these key phrases to identify and index documents that are similar or related. You query these semantic indexes by using three Transact-SQL rowset functions to retrieve the results as structured data. These functions are **SEMANTICKEYPHRASETABLE**, **SEMANTICSIMILARITYTABLE**, **SEMANTICSSIMILARITYDETAILSTABLE**.

For example, consider the following T-SQL statement using the new **SEMANTICSSIMILARITYDETAILSTABLE** function:

SET @SourceTitle = 'first.docx'

SET @MatchedTitle = 'second.docx'

SELECT @SourceDocID = DocumentID FROM Documents WHERE DocumentTitle = @SourceTitle

SELECT @MatchedDocID = DocumentID FROM Documents WHERE DocumentTitle = @MatchedTitle

SELECT @SourceTitle AS SourceTitle, @MatchedTitle AS MatchedTitle, keyphrase, score

   FROM SEMANTICSSIMILARITYDETAILSTABLE(Documents, DocumentContent,

```
@SourceDocID, DocumentContent, @MatchedDocID)
    ORDER BY score DESC
```

The previous query gets the key phrases that make the 2 sample documents similar or related to one another. It presents the results in descending order by the score that ranks the weight of each key phrase.

In another example using **SEMANTICSIMILARITYTABLE** you can find similar or related documents. Consider the following T-SQL statements:

```
SET @Title = 'Sample Document.docx'

SELECT @DocID = DocumentID
    FROM Documents
    WHERE DocumentTitle = @Title

SELECT @Title AS SourceTitle, DocumentTitle AS MatchedTitle,
        DocumentID, score
    FROM SEMANTICSIMILARITYTABLE(Documents, *, @DocID)
    INNER JOIN Documents ON DocumentID =
matched_document_key
    ORDER BY score DESC
```

The previous query gets the documents that were identified as similar or related to the sample document.

Before you can index documents with Semantic Search, you have to store the documents in a SQL Server database. Semantic Search can make use of the FileTable feature mentioned in the previous section.

As you can see from the above examples, Semantic Search enables new scenarios that extend beyond well beyond keyword searches.

Management Studio Enhancements

SQL Server Management Studio has been improved in SQL Server 2012. Users may notice a faster load time, multiple monitor support, and other niceties like working with the SQL Server log files offline. In addition to debugging SQL Server stored procedures and functions in SQL Server 2005 SP2 and above, users can now set conditional breakpoints such as IsTrue and HasChanged. Also, there is a T-SQL expression evaluation window that includes the ability to watch data values while debugging.

Breakthrough Insight

There is no question that the amount of data that is generated, consumed, mined, and analyzed is increasing year over year. These data are coming from structured, unstructured and even cloud sources. Your customers are demanding new insights into this data. SQL Server 2012 brings a plethora of new tools and capabilities to help with rapid data exploration and visualization. This release builds upon the extensive BI capabilities in SQL Server 2008 R2 and provides a self-service BI environment that empowers IT with the ability to easily manage.

Rapid data discovery with Power View

Power View is an interactive ad-hoc web-based data exploration and visualization tool designed for users of all levels. This tool is a feature of SQL Server Reporting Services that is integrated within SharePoint and allows users to create powerful immersive reports. Some of the capabilities of a Power View report include single click data transformations and timed animation sequences. The following figure shows a screen shot of a report showing car sales versus the cost of gas.

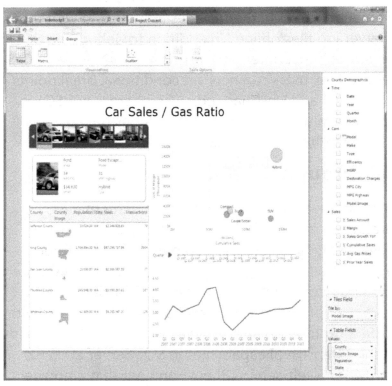

What is displayed in the above screen shot is interactive. If you click on another car the report gets updated in real time. If you click the play button on the timeline graph the data points move along the graph showing their value for that given time. The measures you can select from are defined for the user to quickly access the data. They are not simply relational tables or complex analysis services measures exposed in a tree view for the user to figure out on their own.

With Power View you can have multiple views, up to five, per report. In addition you can export your report to PowerPoint. These reports within PowerPoint are not static; they are interactive just as if you were accessing the report through the tool.

Power View is integrated with SharePoint. Doing so aligns with self-service BI theme where users focus on creating high value content and IT manages the security and compliance of the information. Power View also produced preview images in the PowerPivot Gallery similar to Excel workbooks.

PowerPivot's advanced analytic capabilities

The relatively small row limit of Excel suddenly vanished with the introduction of Power Pivot in SQL Server 2008. Business analysts could now process workbooks with millions of rows with data sourced from a myriad of sources including other reporting services reports. Power Pivot in SQL Server 2012 introduces new analytic capabilities such as creating KPI's, rank, perspectives, hierarchies and complex business logic. Power Pivot also extends the list of Data Analysis Expressions (DAX).

One model for all end user experiences

The Business Intelligence (BI) Semantic Model is being introduced in Analysis Services in SQL Server 2012. This model is one model for all end user experiences. Reporting, analytics, scorecards, dashboards, and custom applications can all now use one model. All BI tools such as Excel, PowerPivot, and Reporting Services including Power View support this model as well.

If you have made investments in Analysis Services cubes also known as the Unified Dimensional Model or UDM rest assured this model is not going away. In fact if you upgrade to SQL Server 2012, every cube automatically becomes a BI Semantic Model.

Respond to data changes with Data Alerts

SQL Server Reporting Services reports can be rendered to the new Office formats for Word and Excel, as well as PDF, TIFF, and HTML. As with previous versions of SQL Server Reporting Services, reports can be delivered on demand to the user or to the user via a subscription. In SQL Server 2012 users can also receive a report based on a data alert which they define to occur upon specific data conditions. This flexibility allows these users to tailor alerts and reporting to their own needs enabling them to respond to data changes much quicker.

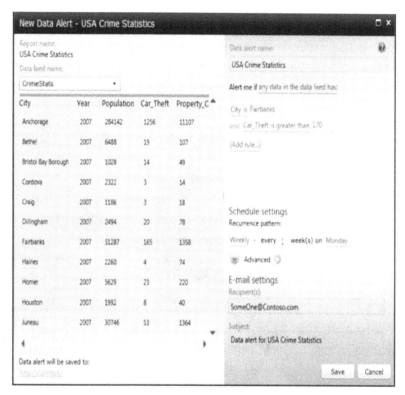

In the above screen shot the user will be sent an alert if car theft is greater than 170 in the city of Fairbanks. Report authors control which data is available for alerting.

From an administrative perspective, data alerts in SQL Server Reporting Services are managed through SharePoint. This increases the IT visibility and control and reduces administrative burden.

Deep benefits with SharePoint integration

Both Power View and Reporting Service Data Alerts require Reporting Services to leverage Sharepoint mode. By doing this, you are reducing the administrative burden and improving the TCO for SharePoint administrators. Tasks like Reporting Services administration, configuration and management can be optionally included in SharePoint 2010 Central Administration Portal.

The setup and installation of Report Services in SharePoint mode is significantly easier. Reporting Services is now optionally installed as a SharePoint shared service application. This provides built-in scale out for reporting services service applications, SharePoint cross-farm reporting and integrated backup and recovery.

Credible data with Data Quality Services

With SQL Server 2012 Data Quality Services data stewards can create and maintain a Data Quality Knowledge Base that will ease data management and improve data quality. Users can use organizational knowledge to profile, cleanse and match data. Data can be validated and cleansed through Windows Azure Marketplace DataMarket services as well. Data Quality Services can be run standalone or in conjunction with SQL Server Integration Services.

Easy management of Master Data Structures

An organizations master data may contain object mapping, reference data, and dimension and hierarchies. SQL Server 2008 R2 introduced SQL Server Master Data Services (MDS). SQL Server 2012 builds upon this by making it really easy to manage the member and attribute values. Now there is an MDS Add-in for Excel so now information workers can build data management applications leveraging MDS data right in Excel.

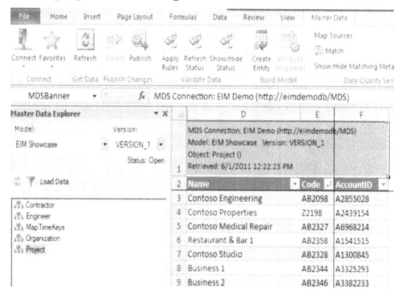

MDS includes an overhauled user experience for Explorer and Integration Management capabilities. User can add and delete more quickly and easily move members within a hierarchy.

What's new in SQL Server Integration Services

SQL Server 2012 contains a plethora of improvements. Designer usability improvements include tutorials and undo/redo on the designer surface. The Scripting component has been upgraded to VSTA 3.0 which means it gives support for .NET version 4.0. Script debugging is also supported within the script tasks.

The SSIS package format is also human readable and can easily be compared with other packages.

Microsoft partnered with Attunity and in addition to bringing in native ODBC source and destination components, Attunity provides some great Change Data Capture (CDC) functionality out of the box. This includes a CDC Control Task, a CDC Source component, and a CDC Splitter transform (that splits the output based on the CDC operation – insert/update/delete). There also exists CDC support for Oracle.

Perhaps the biggest change with SSIS in SQL Server 2012 is the introduction of a new package deployment model. With this model, you can deploy a project to an SSIS server and leverage parameters within packages and projects. Since SSIS in SQL Server 2012 makes good use of the Visual Studio project concept, it's much more useful now to leverage build configurations within your SSIS deployments. With the combination of build configurations and parameters you can easily set a group of parameter values when connected to a test server and another different set of parameter values when connecting to a production server.

What's new in Analysis Services

There are a plethora of new features within SQL Server Analysis Services enough to probably fill another book this size. Some of these advancements include row level security, resource usage reporting, PowerShell for AMO and many others. SQL Server Analysis Services can also be sysprepped in SQL Server 2012. Check out the following link for more info: http://msdn.microsoft.com/en-us/library/bb522628(v=sql.110).aspx.

Cloud on Your Terms

There is no doubt that cloud computing has been a hot topic for most customers over the past few years. Microsoft has made many investments across Windows Server and SQL Server to provide the best cloud-ready information platform available. Whether you are interested in building a private cloud environment or leveraging the public cloud for its elastic computing power, Microsoft has a solution to scale on demand with flexible deployment options to fit your needs.

Building a SQL Server Private Cloud

The first step in building a private cloud is to consider what databases will reside in this new environment. Most customers build a private cloud to consolidate and virtualize databases. If this is one of your goals, the first step is to determine your entire SQL Server footprint. To help with this data gathering exercise, Microsoft provides a free tool called the Microsoft Assessment and Planning Toolkit (MAPS) that helps you inventory your SQL Server environment in addition to other assets. Information obtained from this tool are things like server name, edition, service pack level, free disk space, memory, number of cores, databases, users, and many others. The MAPS tool can be downloaded from http://www.microsoft.com/map.

Most customers who build a private cloud leverage server virtualization. Microsoft Virtual Machine Manager 2012 is a cloud management tool that allows you to perform physical to virtual migrations, cloud service deployments, and many other tasks needed to a manage a cloud infrastructure. For more information on VMM 2012 check out http://www.microsoft.com/scvmm.

One of the main benefits of developing a SQL Server private cloud environment is the ability to scale resources efficiently. By using SQL Server 2012 in conjunction with Windows Server Hyper-V you enable much efficiency. Suppose you had a lot of SQL Server databases that were not used that much. Rather than allocating a lot of RAM to each of these virtual machines, administrators can initially set the virtual machine to run with minimal RAM. As the virtual machine is used, SQL Server will request more memory and Hyper-V will allocate RAM up until a limit the administrator specifies. This Hyper-V feature is called dynamic memory.

Microsoft Hyper-V also supports SQL Server guest failover clustering as well as clustering the virtual machine hosts. With Hyper-V live migration, virtual machine hosts running SQL Server can be moved in real time with no downtime. This is perfect for hardware upgrades and other downtime events.

Having self-service capabilities means you can deploy resources on demand. Microsoft ships a self-service web portal and workload provisioning engine that's integrated with System Center. This automated capability takes some of the burden off of IT administrators allowing them to focus their energies on other area.

A SQL Server private cloud can be built using all these products: Windows Server Hyper-V, SQL Server 2012,

Microsoft System Center Virtual Machine Manager 2012, and Microsoft System Center Operations Manager. If you choose to self-build there is a guide to help you. The Hyper-V private cloud deployment guide is located at the following URL: http://www.microsoft.com/en-us/server-cloud/private-cloud/hyperv-cloud-deployment.aspx. The guide walks you through the specific architecture, deployment and operational tasks within building a private cloud.

Making life easier with appliances

In the previous section you learned about the components needed to build your own SQL Server private cloud. If you want more of a plug and play solution, there are a few vendors with SQL Server appliances out in the market.

The HP Enterprise Database Consolidation appliance consolidates and manages thousands of databases, integrates hardware, software and support and is scalable to meet your changing business needs. It is sold in half and full rack configurations allowing you to easily slap on more as you need. The benefit with the appliance is all the components are already installed, preconfigured, and tuned. All you need to do is provision your databases. For more information on the HP Enterprise Database Consolidation Appliance check out the following URL: http://www.microsoft.com/sqlserver/en/us/solutions-technologies/Appliances/HP-dca.aspx.

Sync data between on-premise and the cloud

SQL Azure is Microsoft's database as a service offering. SQL Azure is SQL Server running in a Microsoft data center available to you to leverage similar to as you would with an on-premise SQL Server solution. One of the scenarios where customers leverage SQL Azure is in a hybrid on-premise and public cloud environment. A feature within SQL Azure called SQL Azure Data Sync allows you to synchronize data between a SQL Azure databases and an on-premise SQL Server database. With this capability you can easily share data between various locations. One scenario is when we have a sales database in SQL Azure and a SQL Server database residing on our salespeople's laptop. These data are periodically synchronized with the SQL Azure database containing all the Sales data. Another scenario is where you want to increase the performance of data access across geographic areas. For example, you would like users in China and those in the United States to have the same performance against the database. With SQL Azure data sync the data resides in a data center close to the user.

With SQL Azure Data Sync there is no code needed to do the synchronization. SQL Azure Data Sync is configured and managed through the Windows Azure web portal. It is there where you specify which data sets you want to replicate such as a table or some columns or a certain select few rows. SQL Azure Data Sync also has native conflict resolution capabilities.

For more information check out this overview video on Channel 9: http://channel9.msdn.com/posts/SQL-Azure-Data-Sync-An-Overview.

SQL Server Data Tools (SSDT)

SQL Server Developer Tools is a single development portal that ships with SQL Server 2012 and Visual Studio. The tool allows users to author a complete BI solution or integrate data across databases and platforms. With respect to SQL Server, SSDT has an add-on that can be downloaded called Database projects. Database projects provides database developers with code navigation, IntelliSense, language support that parallels what is available for C# and VB, platform specific validation, debugging and declarative editing in the TSQL Editor, as well as a visual Table Designer for both database projects and online database instances. You can also integrate your database projects with Entity Framework projects. When it's time to deploy your project, you can choose to publish to all available SQL platforms, including SQL Azure and SQL Server 2012.

Build once, deploy anywhere

One of the goals of SSDT is to unify database development between on-premise and cloud environments. The idea is write application once, deploy anywhere, scale your business solutions fast. Data-Tier Application Components (dacpacs) are packages that contain the schemas and objects required to support an application. SSDT helps you create dacpacs for relational database applications as well as BI projects. In SQL Server 2012 dacpacs include support for permissions, role memberships, synonyms, CLR system types: HierarchyID, Geometry and Geogrpahy, Spatial index and statistics.

Big Data with SQL Server

The world is filling with structured and unstructured data. Imagine for a moment the indexes that are created by search engines like Google, Yahoo and Bing. These data reach petabyte and Exabyte ranges. With very large datasets like these the cost of regenerating indexes is so high you can't easily index changing data. You will also run into locking issues given the amount of machines trying to write to the database. One of the solutions some companies like Google have been using is Apache Hadoop. Apache Hadoop is not a database, rather it's a Java based distributed computing platform. Here the idea is not of a relational database, rather, vaguely-related files in a distributed file system. Microsoft supports Hadoop by publishing a connector for SQL Server to interact with Hadoop. Users can transfer data between Hadoop and SQL Server and between Hadoop and the SQL Server Parallel Data Warehouse appliance. These allow their Microsoft Enterprise Data Warehouses and Business Intelligence solutions to gain deeper business insights from both structured and unstructured data. For more information on the Apache Hadoop connector check out the following URL:
http://www.microsoft.com/download/en/details.aspx?id=2 7584.

Where to learn more

The starting point for general SQL Server information is http://www.microsoft.com/sqlserver. For technical information SQL Server Books Online is a great resource to use. It is located at the following URL: http://msdn.microsoft.com/en-us/library/ms130214%28v=sql.110%29.aspx.

For virtual labs check out the SQL Server Virtual Labs located at the following URL: http://www.microsoft.com/sqlserver/en/us/learning-center/virtual-labs.aspx. As of the time of this writing there are labs for AlwaysOn, PowerView, Distributed Replay, Upgrading to SQL Server 2012 and many more.

Appendix A: Features by Edition

The following section lists the features that are supported by each of the three core editions:

Cross-Box Scale Limits

Feature	Enterprise	BI	Standard
Maximum Compute Capacity Used by a Single Instance**(Database Engine)**	Operating System Maximum	Limited to lesser of 4 Sockets or 16 cores	Limited to lesser of 4 Sockets or 16 cores
Maximum Compute Capacity Used by a Single Instance **(Analysis Services, Reporting Services)**	Operating System Maximum	Operating System Maximum	Limited to lesser of 4 Sockets or 16 cores
Maximum memory utilized **(SQL Server Database Engine)**	Operating System Maximum	64 GB	64 GB
Maximum memory utilized **(Analysis Services)**	Operating System Maximum	Operating System Maximum	64 GB
Maximum memory utilized **(Reporting Services)**	Operating System Maximum	Operating System Maximum	64 GB
Maximum relational Database size	524 PB	524 PB	524 PB

High Availability (AlwaysOn)

Feature	Enterprise	BI	Standard
Server Core support	Yes	Yes	Yes
Log Shipping	Yes	Yes	Yes
Database mirroring	Yes	Yes (Safety Full Only)	Yes (Safety Full Only)
Failover Clustering	Yes (OS maximum)	2 node only	2 node only
Backup compression	Yes	Yes	Yes
Database snapshots	Yes	--	--
AlwaysOn AvailabilityGroups	Yes	--	--
SQL Server multi-subnet clustering	Yes	--	--
Connection Director	Yes	--	--
Online page and file restore	Yes	--	--
Online indexing	Yes	--	--
Online schema change	Yes	--	--
Fast recovery	Yes	--	--
Mirrored Backups	Yes	--	--
Hot add memory and CPU	Yes	--	--

Scalability and Performance

Feature	Enterprise	BI	Standard
Multi-instance support	50	50	50
Table and index partitioning	Yes	--	--
Data compression	Yes	--	--
Resource Governor	Yes	--	--
Partition Table Parallelism	Yes	--	--
Multiple Filestream containers	Yes	--	--

Security

Feature	Enterprise	BI	Standard
Basic auditing	Yes	Yes	Yes
Fine Grained Auditing	Yes	--	--
Transparent database encryption	Yes	--	--
Extensible Key Management	Yes	--	--

Replication

Feature	Enterprise	BI	Standard
SQL Server Change Tracking	Yes	Yes	Yes
Merge Replication	Yes	Yes	Yes
Transactional Replication	Yes	Yes	Yes
Snapshot replication	Yes	Yes	Yes
Heterogeneous subscribers	Yes	Yes	Yes
Oracle publishing	Yes	--	--
Peer to Peer transactional replication	Yes	--	--

Management Tools

Feature	Enterprise	BI	Standard
SQL Management Objects	Yes	Yes	Yes
SQL Configuration Manager	Yes	Yes	Yes
SQLCMD (command prompt tool)	Yes	Yes	Yes

SQL Server Management Studio	Yes	Yes	Yes
Distributed Replay – Admin Tool & Client	Yes	Yes	Yes
Distributed Replay – Controller	Yes (Enterprise supports up to 16 clients, Developer edition supports 1)	Yes (1 client support only)	Yes (1 client support only)
SQL Profiler	Yes	Yes	Yes
SQL Server Agent	Yes	Yes	Yes
Microsoft System Center Operations Manager Management Pack	Yes	Yes	Yes
Database Tuning Advisor	Yes	Yes	Yes

Relational database manageability

Feature	Enterprise	BI	Standard
Dedicated Admin Connection	Yes	Yes	Yes
Powershell Scripting	Yes	Yes	Yes
SysPrep support	Yes	Yes	Yes

Support for Data-tier application component operations	Yes	Yes	Yes
Policy automation	Yes	Yes	Yes
Performance Data Collector	Yes	Yes	Yes
Ability to enroll as a managed instance	Yes	Yes	Yes
Standard performance reports	Yes	Yes	Yes
Plan guides, plan freezing	Yes	Yes	Yes
Direct query of indexes views (using NOEXPAND hint)	Yes	Yes	Yes
Automatic indexed view maintenance	Yes	Yes	Yes
Distributed partitioned views	Yes	Partial. Distributed Partitioned Views are not updatable.	Partial. Distributed Partitioned Views are not updatable.
Parallel indexed operations	Yes	--	--

	Enterprise	BI	Standard
Automatic use of indexed view by query optimizer	Yes	--	--
Parallel consistency check	Yes	--	--
SQL Server utility control point	Yes	--	--

Development Tools

Feature	Enterprise	BI	Standard
Microsoft Visual Studio Integration	Yes	Yes	Yes
SQL Server Developer Studio	Yes	Yes	Yes
Intellisence (Transact-SQL and MDX)	Yes	Yes	Yes
SQL Server Data Tools (SSDT)	Yes	Yes	Yes
SQL query edit and design tools	Yes	Yes	Yes
Version control support	Yes	Yes	Yes
MDX edit, debug and design tools	Yes	Yes	Yes

Programmability

Feature	Enterprise	BI	Standard
Common Language Runtime (CLR) Integration	Yes	Yes	Yes
Native XML support	Yes	Yes	Yes
XML indexing	Yes	Yes	Yes
MERGE and UPSERT	Yes	Yes	Yes
FILESTREAM support	Yes	Yes	Yes
FileTable	Yes	Yes	Yes
Date and Time datatypes	Yes	Yes	Yes
Internationalization support	Yes	Yes	Yes
Full text semantic search	Yes	Yes	Yes
Specification of language in query	Yes	Yes	Yes
Service Broker (messaging)	Yes	Yes	Yes
Web services (HTTP/SOAP) endpoints	Yes	Yes	Yes
T-SQL endpoints	Yes	Yes	Yes

SQL Server Integration Services

Feature	Enterprise	BI	Standard
SQL Server Import and Export Wizard	Yes	Yes	Yes
Built-in data source connectors	Yes	Yes	Yes
SSIS designer and runtime	Yes	Yes	Yes
Basic transforms	Yes	Yes	Yes
Basic data profiling tools	Yes	Yes	Yes
High performance Oracle destination	Yes	--	--
High performance Teradata destination	Yes	--	--
SAP BW source and destination	Yes	--	--
Data mining model training destination adapter	Yes	--	--
Dimension processing destination adapter	Yes	--	--
Partition processing destination adapter	Yes	--	--
Persistent (high performance) lookups	Yes	--	--

Feature	Enterprise		
Data mining query transformation	Yes	--	--
Fuzzy grouping and lookup transformations	Yes	--	--
Term extractions and lookup transformations	Yes	--	--

Master Data Services

Master Data Services is available on the 64-bit editions of Enterprise and Business Intelligence editions only.

Feature	Enterprise	BI	Standard
Master Data Services database	Yes	Yes	--
Master Data Manager web application	Yes	Yes	--

Data Warehouse

Feature	Enterprise	BI	Standard
Create cube without a database	Yes	Yes	Yes
Auto-generate staging and data warehouse schema	Yes	Yes	Yes
Change data capture	Yes	--	--

Star join query optimizations	Yes	--	--
Scalable read-only Analysis Services configuration	Yes	--	--
Proactive caching	Yes	--	--
Parallel query processing on partitioned tables and indicies	Yes	--	--
ColumnStore indexes	Yes	--	--

Analysis Services

Feature	Enterprise	BI	Standard
Scalable Shared Databases (Attach/Detach, read only)	Yes	Yes	--
High availability	Yes	Yes	Yes
Programmability (AMO, ADOMD.Net, OLEDB, XML/A, ASSL)	Yes	Yes	Yes

BI Semantic Model (Multidimensional)

Feature	Enterprise	BI	Standard
Semi-additive measures	Yes	Yes	--

Hierarchies	Yes	Yes	Yes
KPIs	Yes	Yes	Yes
Perspectives	Yes	Yes	--
Actions	Yes	Yes	Yes
Account intelligence	Yes	Yes	Yes
Time intelligence	Yes	Yes	Yes
Custom rollups	Yes	Yes	Yes
Writeback cube	Yes	Yes	Yes
Writeback dimensions	Yes	Yes	--
Writeback cells	Yes	Yes	Yes
Drill through	Yes	Yes	Yes
Advanced hierarchy types (Parent-child, ragged hierarchies)	Yes	Yes	Yes
Advanced dimensions (reference dimensions, many-to-many)	Yes	Yes	Yes
Linked measures and dimensions	Yes	Yes	--
Translations	Yes	Yes	--
Aggregations	Yes	Yes	Yes
Multiple partitions	Yes	Yes	Yes up to 3

Proactive caching	Yes	Yes	--
Custom assemblies	Yes	Yes	Yes
MDX queries and scripts	Yes	Yes	Yes
Role-based security model	Yes	Yes	Yes
Dimension and cell-level security	Yes	Yes	Yes
Scalable string storage	Yes	Yes	Yes
MOLAP, ROLAP, HOLAP storage modes	Yes	Yes	Yes
Binary and compressed XML transport	Yes	Yes	Yes
Push-mode processing	Yes	Yes	--
Direct writebacks	Yes	Yes	--
Measure Expressions	Yes	Yes	--

BI Semantic Model (Tabular)

Feature	Enterprise	BI	Standard
Semi-additive measures	Yes	Yes	--
Hierarchies	Yes	Yes	--

KPIs	Yes	Yes	--
Perspectives	Yes	Yes	--
Translations	Yes	Yes	--
DAX calculations, DAX queries, MDX queries	Yes	Yes	--
Row-level security	Yes	Yes	--
Partitions	Yes	Yes	--
VertiPaq and DirectQuery storage modes (Tabular only)	Yes	Yes	--

PowerPivot for SharePoint

Feature	Enterprise	BI	Standard
SharePoint farm integration based on shared service architecture	Yes	Yes	--
Usage reporting	Yes	Yes	--
Health monitoring rules	Yes	Yes	--
PowerPivot Gallery	Yes	Yes	--
PowerPivor Data Refresh	Yes	Yes	--
PowerPivot Data Feeds	Yes	Yes	--

Data Mining

Feature	Enterprise	BI	Standard
Standard Algorithms	Yes	Yes	Yes
Data Mining Tools	Yes	Yes	Yes
Cross Validation	Yes	Yes	--
Models of Filtered Subsets of Mining Structure Data	Yes	Yes	--
Time Series: Custom Blending Between ARTXP and ARIMA Methods	Yes	Yes	--
Time Series: Prediction with New Data	Yes	Yes	--
Unlimited Concurrent DM Queries	Yes	Yes	--
Advanced Configuration & Tuning	Yes	Yes	--
Support for plug-in algorithms	Yes	Yes	--
Parallel Model Processing	Yes	Yes	--

Time Series: Cross-Series Prediction	Yes	Yes	--
Unlimited attributes for Association Rules	Yes	Yes	--
Sequence Prediction	Yes	Yes	--
Multiple Prediction Targets for Naïve Bayes, Nueral network and logistic regression	Yes	Yes	--

Reporting Services

Feature	Enterprise	BI	Standard
Supported catalog DB SQL Server edition	Standard or higher	Standard or higher	Standard or higher
Supported data source SQL Server edition	All SQL Server editions	All SQL Server editions	All SQL Server editions
Report Server	Yes	Yes	Yes
Report Designer	Yes	Yes	Yes
Report Manager	Yes	Yes	Yes
Role based security	Yes	Yes	Yes
Word export and rich text support	Yes	Yes	Yes

Enhanced gauges and charting	Yes	Yes	Yes
Export to Excel, PDF and image formats	Yes	Yes	Yes
Custom authentication	Yes	Yes	Yes
Report as data feed	Yes	Yes	Yes
Model support	Yes	Yes	Yes
Create custom roles for role-based security	Yes	Yes	Yes
Model Item security	Yes	Yes	Yes
Infinite click through	Yes	Yes	Yes
Shared component library	Yes	Yes	Yes
Email and file share subscriptions and scheduling	Yes	Yes	Yes
Report history, execution snapshots and caching	Yes	Yes	Yes
SharePoint integration	Yes	Yes	Yes
Remote and non-SQL data source support	Yes	Yes	Yes

Data source, delivery and rendering, RDCE extensibility	Yes	Yes	Yes
Data driven report subscription	Yes	Yes	--
Scale out deployment (web farms)	Yes	Yes	--
Alerting	Yes	Yes	--
Power View	Yes	Yes	--

Business Intelligence Clients

Feature	Enterprise	BI	Standard
Report Builder	Yes	Yes	Yes
Data Mining Addins for Excel and Visio 2010	Yes	Yes	Yes
PowerPivot for Excel 2010	Yes	Yes	--
Master Data Services Add-in for Excel	Yes	Yes	--

Spatial and Location Services

Feature	Enterprise	BI	Standard
Spatial indexes	Yes	Yes	Yes

Feature			
Planar and Geodetic datatypes	Yes	Yes	Yes
Advanced spatial libraries	Yes	Yes	Yes
Import/export of industry-standard spatial data formats	Yes	Yes	Yes

Other components and database services

Feature	Enterprise	BI	Standard
SQL Server Migration Assistant	Yes	Yes	Yes
Database Mail	Yes	Yes	Yes
Data Quality Services	Yes	Yes	--
Stream Insight	StreamInsight Premium Edition	StreamInsight Standard Edition	StreamInsight Standard Edition
Stream Insight HA	StreamInsight Premium Edition	--	--

Note: Every effort is made to ensure these lists of features per edition are accurate. There may be a time when these change and are not reflected in this text. Please refer to the following URL for the latest information on this topic: http://www.microsoft.com/sqlserver/en/us/editions.aspx.

Appendix B: Licensing Datasheet

The following is a reprint of a portion of the SQL Server 2012 Licensing Datasheet published December 1, 2011 by Microsoft at the following URL: http://www.microsoft.com/sqlserver/en/us/future-editions/sql2012-licensing.aspx. Please check this website for the latest information.

Editions overview

The SQL Server 2012 Editions have been streamlined to better align with how customers are deploying applications and solutions. SQL Server 2012 will be released in 3 main editions*:

- Enterprise for mission critical applications and large scale data warehousing
- Business Intelligence, a new product edition, providing premium corporate and self-service BI
- Standard for basic database, reporting and analytics capabilities

The main editions are now offered in a consistent, tiered model which creates greater consistency across editions, features and licensing. Enterprise Edition will include all features available in SQL Server 2012. The Business Intelligence Edition will include premium BI features as well as all of the Standard Edition features.

*Note: SQL Server 2012 will continue to be available in Developer, Express and Compact editions. Web Edition will be offered in a Services Provider License Agreement (SPLA) model only. Datacenter Edition is being retired with all capabilities now available in Enterprise. Workgroup and Small business Editions are also being retired.

SQL Server 2012 Licensing Options

SQL Server 2012 will continue to offer two licensing options - one based on computing power, and one based on users or devices. In the computing power-based license model, however, the way we measure power will shift from processors to cores. Core-based licensing provides a more precise measure of computing power and a more consistent licensing metric regardless of where the solution is deployed across on-premises, virtual and cloud scenarios.

- Enterprise Edition (EE) will be licensed based on compute capacity measured in cores
- Business Intelligence (BI) Edition will be available in the Server + CAL model, based on users or devices
- Standard Edition (SE) offers both licensing models to address basic database workloads

| SQL Server 2012 Editions | | Description | Licensing Options | | Pricing** |
			Server + CAL	Core Based	Open NL (US$)
Main Editions	Enterprise	High end datacenter, data warehousing and BI capabilities		✓	$6,874 per Core
	Business Intelligence	Enterprise BI and High Scale Analytics	✓		$8,592 per Server*
	Standard	Basic database and BI capabilities	✓	✓	$1,793 per Core, or $898 per Server*
	Client Access License (CAL)	Access to SQL Server databases licensed per server			$209 per CAL

Requires CALs, which are sold separately
**Pricing is for demonstrative uses only*

Core-Based Licensing

The Enterprise Edition and Standard Edition of SQL Server 2012 will both be available under core-based licensing. Core-based licenses will be sold in two-core packs.

Core based licensing is appropriate when customers are unable to count users/devices, have Internet/Extranet facing workloads or systems that integrate with external facing workloads.

To license a physical server, you must license all the cores in the server with a minimum of 4 core licenses required for each physical processor in the server.

Core licenses will be priced at 1/4 the cost of a SQL Server 2008 R2 (EE/SE) processor license.

How to license					
1. License all of the physical cores on the hardware					
2. A minimum of 4 core licenses are required per physical processor					
PHYSICAL CORES IN THE PROCESSOR:	1	2	4	6	8
CORE LICENSES REQUIRED	4	4	4	6	8

Server and Client Access License (CAL) Licensing

The Business Intelligence and Standard Editions will be available under the Server and Client Access License (CAL) model.

This licensing model can be used when the number of users can be readily counted (e.g., internal database applications).

To access a licensed SQL Server, each user must have a SQL Server CAL that is the same version or newer (for example, to access a SQL Server 2008 SE server, a user would need a SQL Server 2008 or 2012 CAL).

Each SQL Server CAL can provide access to multiple licensed SQL Servers, including the new Business Intelligence Edition as well as Standard Edition Servers and legacy Enterprise Edition Servers.
The SQL Server 2012 CAL price will increase by about 27%.

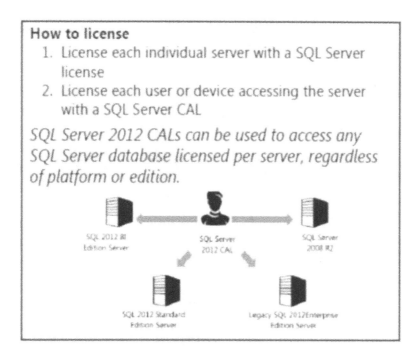

How to license

1. License each individual server with a SQL Server license
2. License each user or device accessing the server with a SQL Server CAL

SQL Server 2012 CALs can be used to access any SQL Server database licensed per server, regardless of platform or edition.

Virtualization Licensing - Cloud Optimized

SQL Server 2012 will offer expanded virtualization rights, options and benefits to provide greater flexibility for customers deploying in virtual environments. There will be two primary virtualization licensing options in SQL Server 2012: The ability to license individual virtual machines and the ability to license for maximum virtualization in highly virtualized and private cloud environments.

Individual Virtual Machines

As hardware capabilities grow, it will become more common for each database to use a fraction of its server's computing power.

When deploying databases on Virtual Machines (VMs) that use just a fraction of a physical server, savings can be achieved by licensing individual VMs.

To license a VM with core licenses, purchase a core license for each virtual core (virtual thread) allocated to the virtual machine (minimum of 4 core licenses per VM).

To license a single VM with a server license (for Business Intelligence or Standard only), buy the server license and buy matching SQL Server CALs for each user.

Each licensed VM covered with Software Assurance (SA) can be moved frequently within a server farm or to a third party hoster or cloud services provider without buying additional SQL Server licenses.

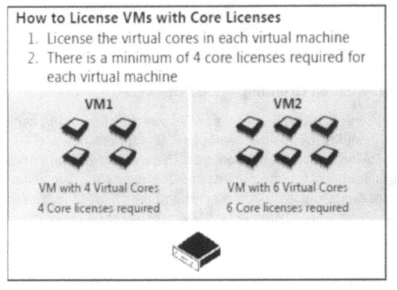

How to License VMs with Core Licenses
1. License the virtual cores in each virtual machine
2. There is a minimum of 4 core licenses required for each virtual machine

VM1

VM with 4 Virtual Cores
4 Core licenses required

VM2

VM with 6 Virtual Cores
6 Core licenses required

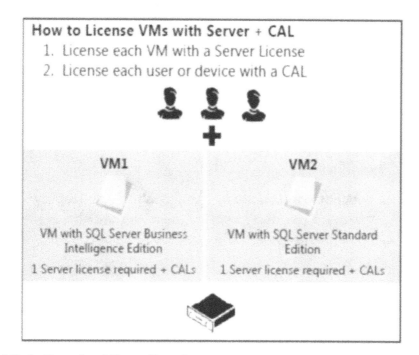

How to License VMs with Server + CAL
1. License each VM with a Server License
2. License each user or device with a CAL

VM1	VM2
VM with SQL Server Business Intelligence Edition	VM with SQL Server Standard Edition
1 Server license required + CALs	1 Server license required + CALs

High Density Virtualization

Further savings can be achieved by operating a database server utility or SQL Server private cloud. This is a great option for customers who want to take advantage of the full computing power of their physical servers and have very dynamic provisioning and de-provisioning of virtual resources.

Customers will be able to deploy an unlimited number of VM's on the server and utilize the full capacity of the licensed hardware.

They can do so by fully licensing the server (or server farm) with Enterprise Edition core licenses and *Software Assurance* based on the total number of physical cores on the servers. SA then enables the ability to run an unlimited number of virtual machines to handle dynamic workloads and fully utilize the hardware¡¦s computing power.

Licensing SQL Server private cloud:

1. License all the physical cores on the server with Enterprise Edition core licenses and SA
2. Deploy an unlimited number of VMs

Example

What you License	What you Deploy
Physical Cores w/EE+SA	Unlimited VMs (example 6)

Single Server, 2 physical processors, 6 cores/processor (12 total)

What to Buy:

12 SQL Server Enterprise Edition core licenses + SA

VM1

VM2

VM3

VM4

VM5

VM6

Transition to the New Licensing Models

In order to facilitate a smooth transition to the new editions and licensing, Microsoft is offering several options. These are designed to help enable customers to plan for the future while protecting their current investments.

Enterprise Edition Server + CAL Licensing

- **New server licenses for SQL Server Enterprise Edition in the Server + Cal model will only be available for purchase through June 30th, 2012, after which they will no longer be available for purchase.** EA/EAP customers that buy SQL Enterprise Edition Servers will have until their next EA/EAP renewal after June 30th, 2012 to purchase additional server licenses to complete currently planned projects. After that, all new SQL Server Enterprise Edition deployments must be purchased per core.

- All existing SQL Server Enterprise Edition licenses under the Server + CAL model with Software Assurance current when SQL Server 2012 launches can be upgraded to SQL Server 2012 at no additional cost, and SA can be maintained (in the server + cal model) to provide access to future software updates. **These Legacy Enterprise Edition Servers remain licensed under the Server + CAL model and require the appropriate version of the SQL Server CAL for users or devices.**

- Legacy SQL Server 2012 Enterprise Edition Server deployments licensed in the server + CAL model will be subject to a **20 core per server license maximum**. This core maximum applies both to new server licenses and to prior version server licenses upgraded to 2012 with SA. If you purchased SQL Server 2008 R2 Enterprise Edition in the Server + CAL model with Software Assurance and at the launch of SQL Server 2012 are running on a server with > 20 physical cores, contact your Microsoft representative for help transitioning to the new licensing model.

- Legacy SQL Server 2012 Enterprise Edition Server licenses are still considered licensed under the Server + CAL model but have the new core limit to allow customers to upgrade their existing deployments and have some near term deployment options to finish currently planned projects under the Server + CAL model for the SQL Server Enterprise Edition.
- Moving forward, customers who would have purchased new EE server licenses can: purchase SQL BI server licenses for business intelligence, purchase SQL EE per core for high-scale database or data warehouse, or maintain legacy EE server licenses for existing projects requiring 20 cores or less.

SQL Server Processor licenses under SA moving to Core-based Licensing

Customers with processor licenses under SA can upgrade to SQL Server 2012 at no additional cost. At the end of the SA term, processor licenses will be exchanged for core licenses and customers can renew their SA on core licenses.

SQL Enterprise and Standard processor licenses under SA will be exchanged for a minimum of 4 core licenses per processor or for the actual number of cores in use. SQL Server Datacenter processor licenses will be exchanged for a minimum of 8 EE core licenses per processor or for the actual number of cores in use.

At the end of the current agreement term, customers should do a self-inventory of systems currently running SQL Server, documenting the number of cores in each processor in use with a SQL Server processor license covered with Software Assurance. This will enable customers to receive the appropriate number of core licenses based on SQL Server 2012 to continue their current deployments.

Customers should do this self-inventory using the Microsoft Assessment and Planning (MAP) Toolkit or other inventory tools and processes to accurately archive a time/date stamped inventory of hardware tied to SQL Server installations.

If customers do not perform the self-inventory, they will receive 4 core licenses for each Standard and Enterprise Edition processor and 8 EE core licenses per Datacenter Edition processor.

PHYSICAL CORES IN THE PROCESSOR:	2	4	6	8	10
ENTERPRISE OR STANDARD – CORES GRANTED	4	4	6	8	10
DATACENTER – EE CORES GRANTED	8	8	8	8	10

License Transition Summary

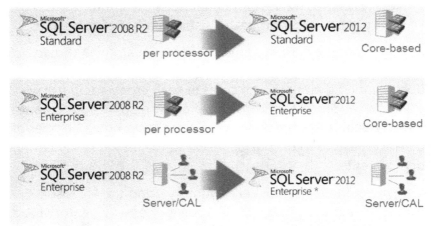

Restricted to servers with no more than 20 cores, New purchases available through 6/30/2011 or expiration of EA/EAP with EE Server post 6/30/2011

Customers with Enterprise Agreements

Customers in existing Enterprise Agreements, EAPs and EASs will be able to continue to purchase Enterprise Edition server and processor licenses through the end of their term.

Customers purchasing processor based licenses through the end of their term will continue to need to calculate the number of licenses required for a deployment based on the 2008 R2 processor use rights.

Customers with an EA or EAP do have the option to add core licenses mid-term to their agreement for future purchases and should contact their reseller or Microsoft account team for more information.

All servers licensed with SQL Server 2012 Enterprise Edition server licenses will be subject to the 20 core server limitation.

The same process as outlined above will be followed at the end of term.

Planning for SQL Server 2012

Customers planning to deploy SQL Server 2012, either through upgrades or new licenses, should remember:

Renewing Software Assurance (SA) is the best way to protect investments and provide access to new versions as well as Deployment Planning Services and technical assistance.

EAP will continue to offer customers the best value, including discounts of up to 40% on new EE and BI server licenses.

Customers should select the right edition depending on usage:

Enterprise for mission critical applications and large scale data warehousing

Business Intelligence for premium corporate and self-service BI

Standard for basic database, reporting and analytics capabilities

Consolidation and virtualization are the best ways to maximize efficiency of hardware and control the size, computing power and more granularly manage cost of your deployments.

Appendix C: Licensing FAQ

The following is a reprint of a portion of the Frequently Asked Questions about SQL Server 2012 Editions and Licensing published by Microsoft at the following URL: http://www.microsoft.com/sqlserver/en/us/future-editions/sql2012-licensing.aspx.   Please check this website for the latest information.

SQL Server 2012 Editions

1. What is new in SQL Server 2012?

SQL Server 2012 will provide Mission Critical Confidence with greater uptime, blazing-fast performance and enhanced security for mission critical workloads; Breakthrough Insight with managed self-service data exploration and stunning interactive data visualizations capabilities; Cloud On Your Terms by enabling the creation and extension of solutions across on-premises and public cloud.

2. Can you describe the product editions offered with SQL Server 2012?

Three main editions, namely Enterprise, Business Intelligence and Standard, will be available:

- Enterprise for mission critical applications and data warehousing
- Business Intelligence (new) for premium corporate and self-service Business Intelligence capabilities
- Standard for basic database capabilities, reporting and analytics

The Business Intelligence edition will include all of the Standard Edition¡¦s capabilities, and Enterprise will include all of the Business Intelligence Edition¡¦s capabilities.

3. What about other editions currently available in SQL Server 2008 R2 such as Datacenter, Workgroup and Standard for Small Business Editions?

With the release of SQL Server 2012, the following three editions will be retired:

- Datacenter - its features will now be available in Enterprise Edition
- Workgroup - Standard will become our edition for basic database needs
- Standard for Small Business - Standard becomes our sole edition for basic database needs

4. What is the full list of editions that will be available with SQL Server 2012?

Enterprise, Business Intelligence and Standard will be our main editions. The Web Edition will be offered only to hosters via the Services Provider License Agreement (SLPA). Developer, Express and Compact Editions will also continue to be distributed without licensing or pricing changes. We also offer a range of appliances including Parallel Data Warehouse, a BI appliance, and a database consolidation appliance.

SQL Server 2012 Licensing

5. What are the key licensing changes with SQL Server 2012?

With SQL Server 2012, we will offer the following licensing options:

- Core-based Licensing for Enterprise
- Server + CAL licensing for Business Intelligence

SQL Server 2012 Pocket Guide   **95**

- Choice of core-based licensing or Server + CAL licensing for Standard

6. When will these changes come into effect?

Licensing changes will come into effect at the general availability of SQL Server 2012. Microsoft SQL Server 2012 is expected to release in the first half of calendar year 2012.

7. Are there any virtualization or cloud-related licensing benefits with SQL Server 2012?

SQL Server 2012 will provide a variety of virtualization and cloud benefits that will help customers save money on database licensing and retain flexibility in their database deployments. Customers can:

- License individual Virtual Machines (VM), and when licensing per core, buy core licenses only for the virtual cores (threads or physical cores) assigned to the VM.
- License for high VM density by buying EE and Software Assurance (SA) for all the physical cores on the server (or server farm) and deploying any number of VMs on the licensed hardware. Without SA, VM density is limited to one VM per core with EE.
- License for VM mobility across private and public clouds. VM license mobility is an SA benefit. Without SA, licenses can be moved from one server to another only once every 90 days.

8. Could you explain why you are making these changes?

The changes to SQL Server licensing reflect the evolution of the database industry along with new hardware deployment practices. Internal customer research with hundreds of customers has shown us that database customers are comfortable with core-based licensing and consider licensing by core simple and predictable. There is also great enthusiasm for our virtualization and cloud-friendly licensing to help customers save money as their deployment practices evolve. With these changes, we will continue to offer industry leading TCO.

9. Will other Microsoft products move to core-based licensing as well?

We have put in place licensing models that are appropriate for the products based on industry and customer needs. The changes to SQL Server licensing are based on trends in the database industry and were developed with just the database business in mind.

10. Will the licensing changes be accompanied by an increase in pricing?

With SQL Server 2012, we are delivering a more powerful Enterprise Edition and a new Business Intelligence Edition with innovative features. SQL Server customers who benefit from the new capabilities and who deploy mission critical databases will likely pay more, though we will continue to be the industry TCO leader.

At the same time, we are offering licensing benefits and flexibility to help customers save money and control costs with virtualization and consolidation. The net price impact to individual customers will vary based on how they deploy SQL Server 2012, their current capacity and their future needs.

We have been actively engaged in conversations directly with our customers and partners to ensure that they know how these changes may impact them.

11. Can I buy core-based licensing for the Business Intelligence edition?

Enterprise Edition includes the full capabilities of SQL Server 2012, so a customer who wants to license a BI Server on a per core basis can do so by buying Enterprise Edition. Enterprise Edition will be the preferred way to license advanced SQL Server BI capabilities when users are uncountable (e.g., external facing workloads) or when there is a very large number of users.

12. Can I use the same CAL for the Business Intelligence and Standard editions?

Yes, as with prior releases, there is a single CAL for SQL Server 2012 for access to all the server editions.

13. I have Software Assurance, do I have to pay more to upgrade to SQL Server 2012?

No. All licenses under SA will be able to upgrade to SQL Server 2012 at no additional cost.

14. I recently signed up for an Enterprise Agreement (EA)/Enrollment for Application Platform (EAP). What do these changes mean for me?

EA and EAP remain the best ways for customers to license SQL Server. EA and EAP offer extended transitions to help you plan for the new licensing model. Furthermore, EAP offers significant discounts to help you take advantage of the lowest TCO.

15. How do I migrate from processor licenses to core licenses? What is the migration path?

Licenses purchased with Software Assurance (SA) will upgrade to SQL Server 2012 at no additional cost. EA/EAP customers can continue buying processor licenses until your next renewal after June 30, 2012. At that time, processor licenses will be exchanged for core-based licenses sufficient to cover the cores in use by processor-licensed databases (minimum of 4 cores per processor for Standard and Enterprise, and minimum of 8 EE cores per processor for Datacenter).

16. How will SQL Server processor licenses with SA be exchanged for SQL Server 2012 core licenses? How will I (and Microsoft) determine the number of cores that I am owed?

You can perform a self-inventory of your environment at the end of the Software Assurance (SA) term that will provide the basis for the core licenses you will own and for which you are eligible to renew SA. We will provide access to the Microsoft Assessment and Planning (MAP) Toolkit as one way to help track and document deployments. This tool can help you plan the transition from processor-based licenses to core-based licenses by counting both processors and cores across your deployments. If you are not able to document your SQL Server deployments, we will exchange processors based on a standard conversion ratio. We encourage you to work with your Microsoft or Partner representative to determine an optimal transition plan.

---

www.ingramcontent.com/pod-product-compliance
Lightning Source LLC
Chambersburg PA
CBHW060948050326
40689CB00012B/2600